BABY LOVE

moments and memories

baby showers

1

To even out the morning sickness, the bizarre cravings and the stretchy pants, pregnancy comes with a few special perks, including one very cool party. Baby showers are a time to celebrate the promise of new life with those you love.

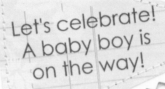

Let's celebrate!
A baby boy is
on the way!

Join us for
a family
celebration

Saturday, April 5th
3:00 p.m.
Bill & Donna's House

Please R.S.V.P. Thanks!

Thanks for coming!
Bill & Donna

Thanks for coming!
Bill & Donna

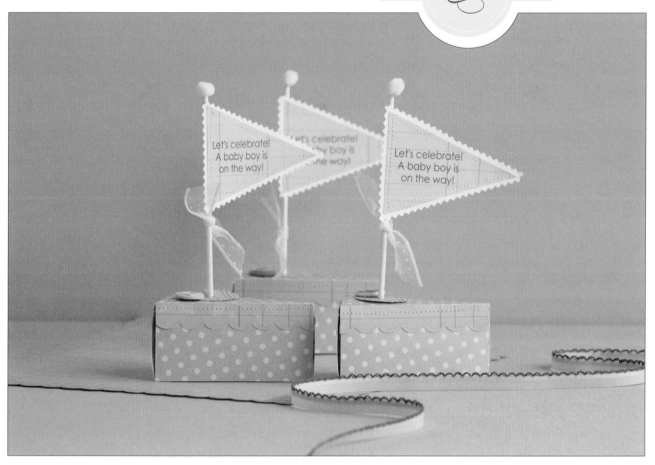

BOATS

1 Print greeting on ledger paper, cut into triangle and adhere to white cardstock

2 Cut cardstock with pinking shears and machine stitch

3 Hot glue flag and white pom pom to lollipop stick, then tie on sheer ribbon

4 Cut triangle box and adhere circle punched from ledger paper to top center of unassembled box

5 Punch hole through center of box and circle, then adhere strips of deco-edge ledger paper and machine stitch

6 Assemble box using adhesive, insert flag stick and hot glue in place inside box

7 Embellish with button

Supplies: fresh anthology buttons, noteworthy papers and trim: Making Memories
Font: Century Gothic
Other: white cardstock, pom poms, lollipop sticks and pinking shears

INVITATION

1 Print greeting on patterned paper

2 Adhere to stripe and ledger papers

3 Machine stitch and add flag

PERSONALIZED CANDIES

1 Remove commercial label, wrap with patterned paper and secure with small pieces of tape

2 Wrap journaling around roll and secure with small pieces of tape

SWEETS

1 Create two 5½" flowers on patterned paper and trim using decorative scissors

2 Take off top part of silk flower down to stem

3 Layer paper and silk flowers together, attaching flower top to stem

4 Curl paper flower petal with pencil and add paper die-cuts to a few flowers

5 Wrap each candy bar with patterned paper, print journaling and attach to front

6 Add tie with ribbon and flower embellishments

GUEST PARTICIPATION

1 Adhere two pieces of patterned paper together, pattern sides facing out

2 Trim patterned paper to 6" x 12", rounding both ends with decorative scissors

3 Using computer, create invitation, adhere on patterned paper and adhere to center of card

4 Score and fold card

5 Trim 1½" strip of patterned paper to wrap around card and tie with ribbon

6 Allow guests to create scrapbook pages by setting out coordinating embellishments

Supplies: garden party paper (dots, stripe and flowers), garden party glitter die-cuts, garden party trims, blossoms (spotlight), garden party dimensional stickers, flower grommets and cheeky white clip: Making Memories
Other: silk flowers

CUPCAKE TOPPERS

1 Create circle tags with ledger paper

2 Stamp images on circle tags

3 Embellish with rhinestones

4 Paint toothpicks and tape to tags

Supplies: tag maker rims (circle large), gem stickers (clear), scrapbook colors acrylic paint (strawberries and cream), foam stamps (baby), ledger paper, tag maker, tag maker punch (circle large): Making Memories
Other: toothpicks

INVITATIONS

1 Create and print invitation

2 Cut out and fit inside baby sock, with 1" exposed

3 Embellish exposed portion with paper, brad and stamp

Supplies: magnetic stamp (ornaments), jumbo pebble brads (pink and brown) and noteworthy paper: Making Memories
Fonts: Helvetica Neue and Susie's Hand
Ink: Color Box Pigment Brush Pad (silver)

NAPKINS

1 Stamp image onto corner of napkin

Supplies: foam stamps (baby) and scrapbook colors acrylic paint (strawberries and cream): Making Memories
Other: napkins

STACKED BOXES

1 Paint boxes, let dry and stamp images onto sides of box
2 Cover tops of lids with paper
3 Cover sides of lids with strips of paper or ribbon
4 Embellish with brads and gem stickers

Supplies: foam stamps (baby), jumbo pebble brads (pink and brown), magnetic stamps (ornaments), ribbon (love 2), valentine pebble brads (love), woven ribbon (sunsoaked), noteworthy paper, scrapbooking colors acrylic paint (strawberries and cream) and gem stickers (clear): Making Memories
Ink: Color Box Pigment Brush Pad (silver)
Other: boxes

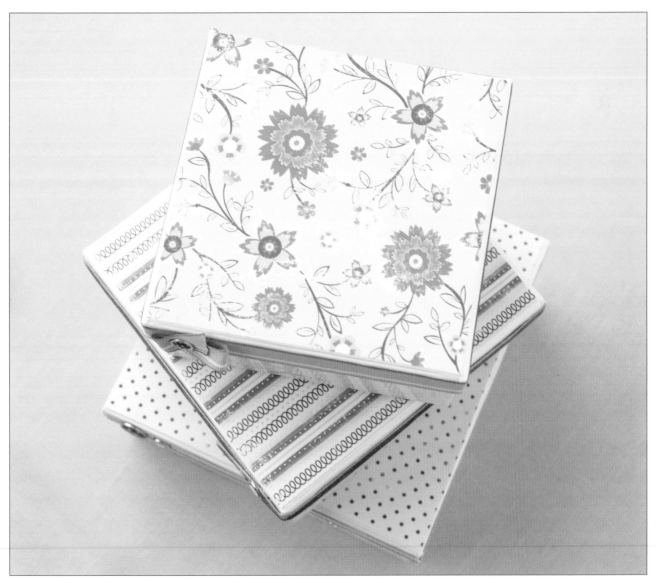

cut thin border using mini scallop deco scissors

INVITATIONS

1 Layer and machine stitch strips of patterned paper on pink cardstock

2 Print invitation on cream cardstock, set on top of stitched card and mark with pencil where slots should be punched

3 Using slot punching tool, punch four slots in card and insert invitation

PARTY FAVOR BOX

1 Die-cut patterned paper to fit box, adhere, then machine stitch two strips of coordinating patterned paper

2 Assemble box using adhesive

3 Wrap ribbon around box and secure on bottom with tape

4 Print label on cream cardstock and punch out using circle punch

5 Mount circle on brown cardstock, cut thin border using mini scallop deco scissors and adhere to front of box

BANNER

1 Adhere and machine stitch squares of patterned paper to brown cardstock
2 Cut cardstock edges using mini scallop deco scissors
3 Mount on pink cardstock and machine stitch around edge
4 Add cheeky clip and tie to pink satin ribbon using wired ribbon and lace

PERSONALIZED CANDY

1 Remove commercial label, wrap with patterned paper and secure with small pieces of tape
2 Wrap journaling around roll and secure with small pieces of tape

Supplies (both pages): cheeky board clips (neutral), dimensional alpha sticker (baby girl), foam brush, scrapbook colors acrylic paint (wisteria), paper (cosmopolitan), slot punching tool and trim: Making Memories
Fonts: Suzanne Quill SH (Courtney) and Copperpl Goth BT
Cardstock: Bazzill
Circle punch: Creative Memories
Deco scissors: Provo Craft
Die: Accucut
Satin and wired ribbon: Offray

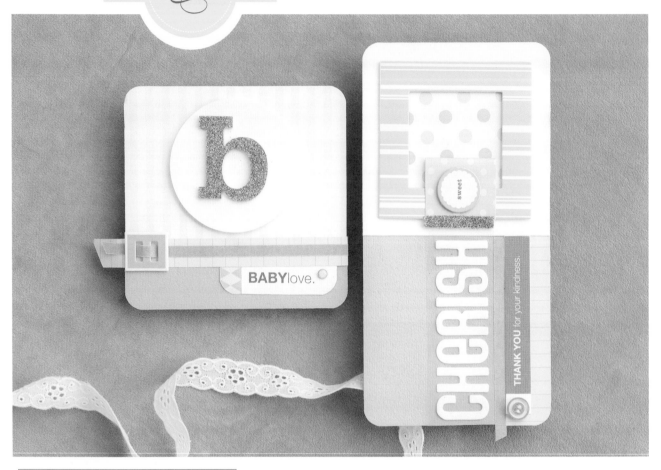

pair coordinated papers and embellishments

BABY LOVE

1 Place light coating of glue on metal letter and sprinkle with green glitter

2 Adhere to white circle and place on striped card

3 Add ribbon to bottom of card with green ribbon accent and place title on bottom right of card

CHERISH

1 Trim green cardstock to a 4" x 8" rectangle

2 Place 'cherish' sticker on left side of card, leaving clear backing in place

3 Print sentiment and adhere

4 Place patterned paper inside frame and accent with folded paper tab and glitter

Supplies (both pages): paper pad (baby boy), metal monogram letter, velvet sayings (wedding), colorboard (baby boy), celery shimmer, fresh anthology buttons, pastel brads (blue and green), pebble brads (springtime), sheer frame (baby), jigsaw poolside, metal frames (holiday 2) and jellies: Making Memories

embellish ribbon with brad accent

BUNDLE OF JOY

1 Trim white cardstock with scallop edged scissors and layer onto polka dot paper

2 Paint chipboard number blue, layering striped paper underneath and add to center of card

3 Place brad through ribbon and adhere under number

4 Print sentiment and adhere below ribbon

CHEERS

1 Back clear frame with dark grey cardstock, placing mini metal frame and number sticker inside

2 Attach ribbon to back of frame, forming a loop

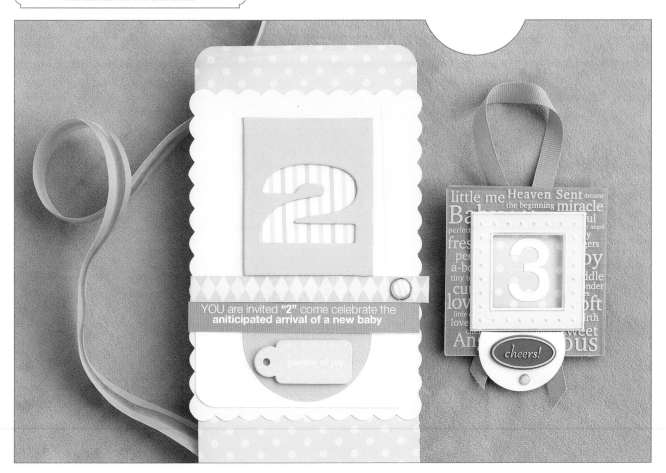

baby announcements

2

Big news can change the world. But that doesn't mean you'll always find it on the front page of the newspaper. Sometimes a special touch is required. That's why, when your world changes, you send out a baby announcement.

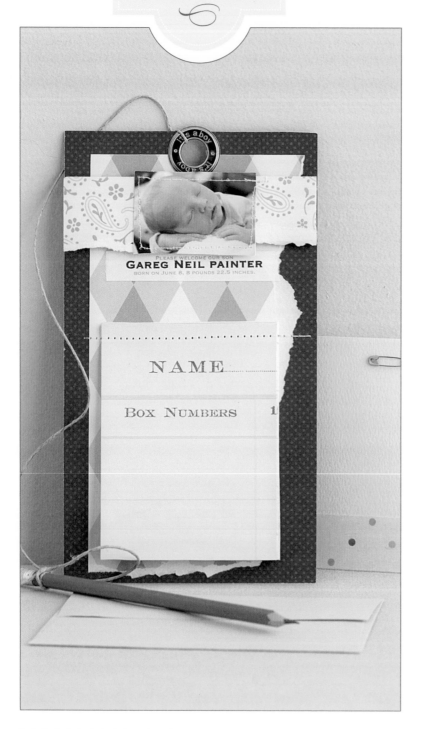

GAREG NEIL PAINTER

PLEASE WELCOME OUR SON
GAREG NEIL PAINTER
BORN ON JUNE 8. 8 POUNDS 22.5 INCHES.

NAME

BOX NUMBERS   1

stitch border around photograph

1 Cut background paper to desired size
2 Embellish with patterned paper and photograph
3 Add grommet and trim
4 Make notepad by cutting ledger paper and stitch to background
5 Attach pencil with string tied to grommet
6 Adhere magnets on back

Supplies: grommets (baby), funky vintage paper (ruby baroque), noteworthy paper (ledger) and scrapbook pad paper (baby boy): Making Memories
Trim: Wal-Mart
Other: pencil

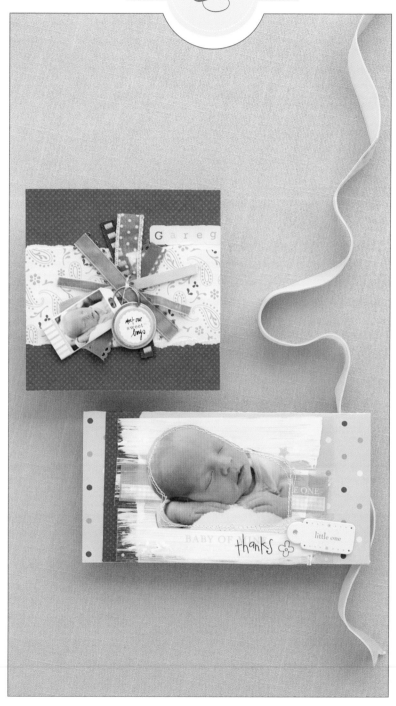

1 Cut square-shaped card from brown patterned paper and fold in half
2 Add paisley strip to background
3 Cut pieces of ribbon and adhere in middle with a stitch
4 Add picture on tag
5 Include details of birth inside card

Supplies: colorboard saying (baby boy), scrapbook pad letter stickers (baby boy), funky vintage paper (ruby baroque), scrapbook pad (baby boy), spring trim, noteworthy trim (audrey), funky vintage trim (lizzie) and fresh anthology trim (eliza): Making Memories Metal tag and blue-green trim: Wal-Mart

attach photo tag and colorboard saying to ring

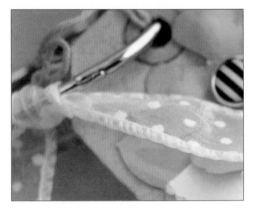

1 Create first tag using cardstock and adhere baby's picture
2 Create second tag by printing birth information on transparency
3 Decorate tags with embellishments
4 Punch holes in tags and connect all three using jump ring
5 Add ribbons to jump ring

Supplies: tropical travel paper (hibiscus), blossom (hibiscus pink/white), buttons (fresh anthology), chipboard buttons (tropical travel), dyed tags (fresh anthology), fresh anthology trim card (eliza), funky vintage trim card (lizzie), pebble brads (black and white), sheer frame combos (baby) and spring trim card (sheer dot white): Making Memories
Transparency: Hambly Screen Print, Other: book rings

a star

is born . . .

attach ribbon pull to birth announcement insert

Jack William Bennett

Born: August 12th 2007
Weight: 7lbs 6 oz.
Length: 21 long

Brother to Kate and Lily
Son to Elizabeth and Jack Sr.

1 Using envelope as template, create pockets from embellishment paper
2 Print information onto white cardstock and attach to printed paper
3 Decorate with ribbon and embellishment and place inside envelope
4 Using photoshop, type words onto picture, print and place on front of pocket envelope
5 Decorate with paper and embellishments

Supplies: tropical travel embellishment paper (palm tree and words), chipboard buttons (tropical travel), funky vintage trim card (lizzie), jigsaw shapes (cheeky): Making Memories

NE
NE
WE
NE
NE
NE
WW
WE

(x)

welcome the twins
(october 14 2007)

2

YOU'VE
TRAVELED
SO FAR
TO BRING

THE NEW ANGEL
congratulations on your new adoption!

add message to interior of card

1 Create cards using a variety of cardstock

2 Print announcement information onto cardstock and attach to card

3 Add embellishments and stickers

Supplies: diamond paper (deck the halls), pebble brads (in bloom), velvet sayings (family stickers), deck the halls colorboard stickers, velvet sayings (baby stickers), rub-ons (black, rummage), letter stickers (mm kids), cheeky clips, vintage hip buttons (gracen), calling cards expression stickers, ledger paper, red and white polka dot border sticker, baby feet, well worn tag (say it), ledger paper, vintage hip button (gracen), kraft paper, nothing but numbers sticker (spotlight) and rub-ons (misunderstood): Making Memories

Font: Pharmacy

Ink: Color Box Pigment Brush Pad (silver)

Other: cardstock and circle punch

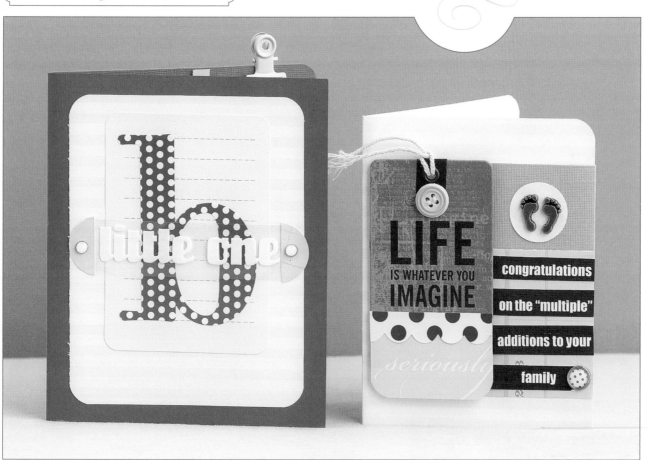

accordion fold announcement

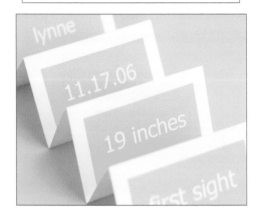

ACCORDIAN

1 Create announcement on computer and print
2 Fold accordion style
3 Cut rectangle of green patterned paper and stitch to white patterned paper
4 Cut slits on either side of where announcement will sit
5 Thread ribbon through slits and tie book in place

PATCHWORK

1 Create announcement on computer and print
2 Attach mini blossoms with button brads

Supplies (both pages): vintage hip trim card (paisley), funky vintage embellishment paper (ruby), brad value packs (buttons black, white and silver) and mini blossoms (neutral and pink): Making Memories
Font: Tahoma

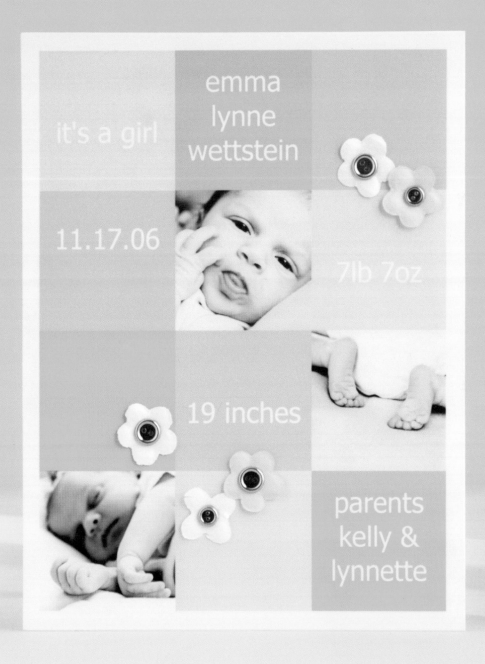

add button rows to cardstock butterflies

1 Stamp star or butterfly image onto cardstock
2 Cover image with shimmer while paint is still wet
3 Once dry, cut out shape and adhere to front of card
4 Embellish with buttons, ribbon and embroidery floss

Supplies: foam stamps (basic shapes and springtime), mini colorboard stickers
(baby boy and baby girl), mm kids trim card (emma), patterned paper (baby, deck the halls
diagonal stripe and noteworthy scallop ledger), scrapbook colors acrylic paint (cornflower
and wisteria), shimmer (aqua blue and lilac) and vintage hip trim card (paisley):
Making Memories
Buttons: Buttons Galore, Cardstock: Bazzill, Embroidery Floss: DMC

1. Layer two squares of cardstock over front of card and sew edges
2. Paint chipboard frame and place on card to trace inner square
3. Using craft knife, trim hole in front of card and adhere frame
4. Embellish card with colorboard stickers, ribbon and brads
5. Place newborn photo inside card

Supplies: button brads (baby boy), jigsaw frames (fresh anthology), mini colorboard stickers (baby boy and baby girl), mm kids trim card (emma and ethan) and scrapbook colors acrylic paint (wisteria): Making Memories
Cardstock: Bazzill

TRANSPARENCY

1 Print layout on transparency film, remembering to print reversed

2 Attach photo, embellishments and ribbon to patterned paper

3 Position transparency over patterned paper and sew together

Supplies: animal crackers paper (jack and ella), button brads (baby girl and baby boy), funky vintage clears alphabet, funky vintage trim cards (lizzie and ruby) and mm kids trim card (max): Making Memories
Other: assorted ribbons, transparency sheets for ink jet printers and thread

LAYERS

1 Use die-cut machine to cut patterned paper into card and attach contrasting paper underneath with double-sided tape

2 Print layout on vellum and adhere to patterned paper with vellum tape

3 Sew around edges of card and attach embellishments

4 Position picture inside card with double-sided tape

Supplies: animal crackers paper (jack and ella) and button brads (baby girl and baby boy): Making Memories
Other: silk ribbon, vellum paper for ink jet printers, thread, double-sided tape and vellum tape

cute as a button

mary·anne
ione
olesen

born 18th
january
2005

4:13am

6 pounds
5 ounces

cute as a button

stitch through embellishments

CARD COLLECTION ALBUM

1 Cover two pieces of cardboard (5" x 9") with patterned paper
2 Add picture and shimmer stickers to front
3 Punch two holes for ring binders and, after aligning, two holes for inner cards, then bind

THANK YOU CARD

1 Cut card from patterned paper
2 Adhere strip of corrugated cardboard with brown paper on top
3 Add embellishments, then stitch across twice

Supplies: funky vintage paper (ruby baroque), scrapbook pad paper (baby girl), shimmer flower stickers (periwinkle) and colorboard sayings (baby girl): Making Memories
Other: corrugated cardboard, machine stitching, cardboard and rings

SQUARE

1 Cut out and layer two cardstock squares, folding the smaller in half

2 Add photograph, sew around photo and embellish with trim tab and brad

DRY ERASE

1 Embellish background cardstock with patterned paper and photo

2 Add grommet, trim and transparency

3 If desired, add magnets on back and use dry erase pen on transparency

Supplies: colorboard saying (baby girl), jumbo brads (pink and brown), funky vintage paper (ruby baroque), scrapbook pad paper (baby girl), spring trim, clear creations (baby), grommets (baby) and noteworthy paper (scalloped circle): Making Memories
Other: white cardstock, dry erase pen and magnet strip

Ezekiel Cheng-Kang Su
February 9, 2007
3:16 pm
6 lbs 7 oz
19¼ inches

1   Trim patterned paper to 4½" x 12", using decorative scissors to round ends

2   Use ribbon slot punch to create notches for photo and place photo in card

3   Score and fold card

4   Create birth announcement on computer and place over photo

5   Trim strip of paper, wrap around card and tie with ribbon

6   Use decorative trim on back of envelope

Supplies: ribbon slot punch, cheeky paper
(dots, gingham and solid) and mm kids trims (max):
Making Memories
Photo credit: Nano Visser

1 Cut paper of choice into card shape
2 Create paper photo frame (trim outside edge with scallop-edged scissors or leave plain)
3 Add names and embellishments

Supplies: silver flower grommet, noteworthy polka dot strip, noteworthy paper (scallop ledger and stamp shape), noteworthy trim card (hillary), noteworthy chipboard alpha, and tiny alpha: Making Memories

gifts for baby

3

They say it's tough to figure out what to get for the person that has everything. But what do you get for the special little person that deserves everything? Make the new bundle in your life coo with delight because of your heartfelt, handmade creations.

group like textures from various product lines

1 Create simple border for inner book pages and type featured word for given page (soft, hard, squishy, rough, etc.)

2 Print out onto white cardstock, sized to fit album of choice, and repeat for each page

3 Adhere printed photograph inside textbox

4 Attach cluster of embellishments and paper to accompany photograph

Supplies: all about alphas (spotlight), cheeky trims (abby), pebble stickers (tropical travel), clears shapes (funky vintage), fabulous flowers (ruby), fresh anthology ribbon (sydney and eliza), funky vintage flocked mini book (chartreuse), heart shimmer stickers and velvet stickers (valentine), fresh anthology jumbo pebble brads (spring 2), pebble brads and shimmer brads (polo club), petals (american and blue and white), ribbons brad (orange and green), shimmer jigsaw alphabets (aqua), shimmer jigsaw shapes (green and purple), simply fabulous velvet alpha (strawberries and cream and asphalt), spring trims and sweets (flowers black and white): Making Memories, Other: book rings

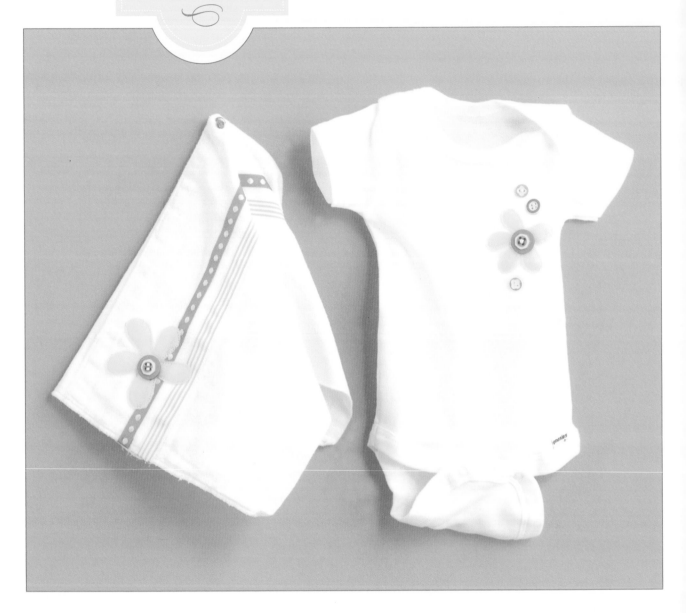

BURP CLOTH

1 Stitch ribbon and felt flower shape to burp cloth

2 Stitch button to center of flower

ONESIE

1 Cut flower shape from felt and stitch to onesie

2 Stitch buttons on securely

Supplies: vintage hip buttons (paisley and gracen) and mm kids trim card (kate): Making Memories

Other: onesie, burp cloth and felt

laminate pages to withstand baby's touch

1 Trace shapes onto patterned paper, cut out and adhere to cardstock squares

2 Cut squares of paper for book cover and add rub-on title

3 Laminate each square, attach eyelet in corners and connect with ring

4 Tie ribbon featuring each color to ring

Supplies: rub-ons alphabet (trademark black), boho chic paper (lauren and olivia), cheeky paper (abby), mm kids paper (emma), simply fabulous paper (brooke), travel paper (orange stripe), deck the halls paper (blue diamond and red check), woven ribbon (sunsoaked), cheeky trim card (abby), fresh anthology trim card (eliza and sydney) and mm kids trim card (bella, emma, sam and ethan): Making Memories

Ribbon: American Crafts, Rub-ons: 7gypsies, Paper (yellow checked): Daisy D's paper (yellow floral): Autumn Leaves

Other: metal ring and large silver eyelets

IRON-ON

1 Using computer word processing or design program, create words, phrases or images

2 Print out on ink-jet printer (don't forget to flip design, so words will read correctly once ironed on)

3 Following manufacturers' instructions, iron design onto onesie

4 Embellish sleeves with ribbon, using washable fabric glue

EMBROIDERED

1 Hand stitch trim securely around sleeves and collar area

2 Create original design or use pattern and embroider onto front of onesie (use tear away stabilizer underneath design)

Supplies: woven ribbon (black and white) and vintage hip trims (gracen): Making Memories
Onesies: Oldnavy.com
Other: embroidery thread, crochet thread, flannel, petite trim and fabric glue

include washing instructions on gift card

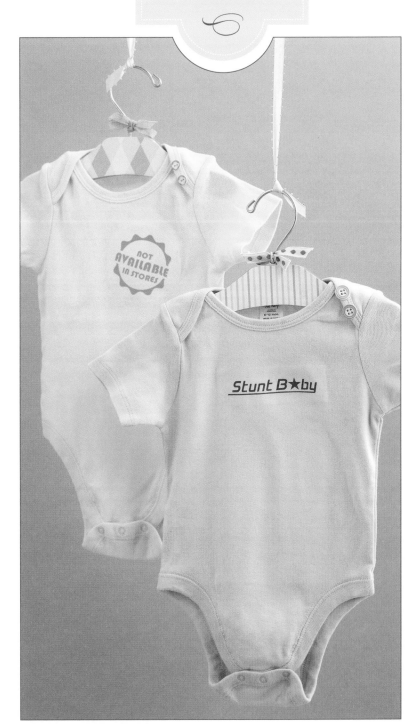

make sure buttons are securely attached

1 Using computer word processing or design
   program, create words, phrases or images

2 Print out on ink-jet printer
   (don't forget to flip design, so words will
   read correctly once ironed on)

3 Following manufacturers' instructions,
   iron design onto onesie

4 Sew buttons onto collar

Supplies: vintage hip buttons: Making Memories
Onesies: Oldnavy.com
Iron-on sheets: Office Depot

1 Cut cards to fit A2 envelopes (4¼" x 5½") or to desired size

2 Embellish cards with self-adhesive textured tape

3 Accent cards with small embellishment, such as a button, small safety pin
   or monogram

Supplies: A2 envelopes (sherbet and springtime), cityscape cardstock (manila), fresh
anthology buttons, paper trimmer, pebble alphabet tags (baby boy), rub-ons book
(alphabet variety 2), safety pins (pastel), springtime cardstock, textured tape (baby
girl and baby boy) and universal glue: Making Memories

1 Trim paper to desired frame size and cut out opening for photo

2 Embellish with decorative edged paper borders or trim

Supplies: fresh anthology paper (eliza dots and spotty flower), mm kids paper (max gingham), noteworthy paper (die-cut ric-rac ledger), springtime lilac paper and ribbon for cards (manila/shopping bag): Making Memories

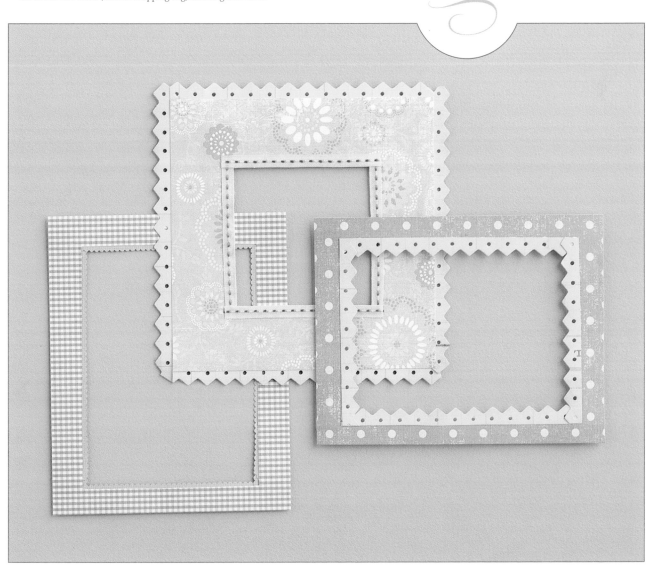

create suitcase tag from leftover supplies

1 Cut paper to fit top of small suitcase

2 Create names and titles with shimmer stickers and embellish

3 Add photos, clear creations and embellishments

4 Cut scalloped circle paper in half and adhere to top of larger suitcase

5 Embellish with velvet stickers and photos

6 Create tag from remaining paper and add journaling, trims and ribbon brads

Supplies: dark pink/light pink ribbon brads, gem stickers (brooke), die-cut stamp shape (hillary), die-cut scalloped circle (audrey), cheeky shimmer stickers (blue and pink), fresh anthology buttons, velvet sayings (baby and all girl), tiny alpha stickers (sherbet), daisy blossoms and clear creations baby book: Making Memories

Other: mini suitcases

attach small tag with mini safety pin

PINK

1 Adhere buttons to center of flowers, then add double-sided flower stickers and shimmer

2 Tie green ribbon around top of hanger and add small tag with mini safety pin

BLUE

1 Use die-cut stamp shape paper to match shape of hanger, adhere and add journaling

2 Tie pink lace around top of hanger

3 Add journaling to small tag and attach with mini safety pin

GREEN

1 Add jewels to center of each dot on hanger

2 Tie pink ribbon around top of hanger and through pink sweet baby tag

Supplies: gem stickers (brooke, maddi and meg), die-cut stamp paper (hillary), die-cut scalloped paper (audrey), sweets tags (baby), spring trims, shimmer spring kit, basic buttons and flower double-sided stickers (glitter): Making Memories

Other: baby hangers and mini safety pins

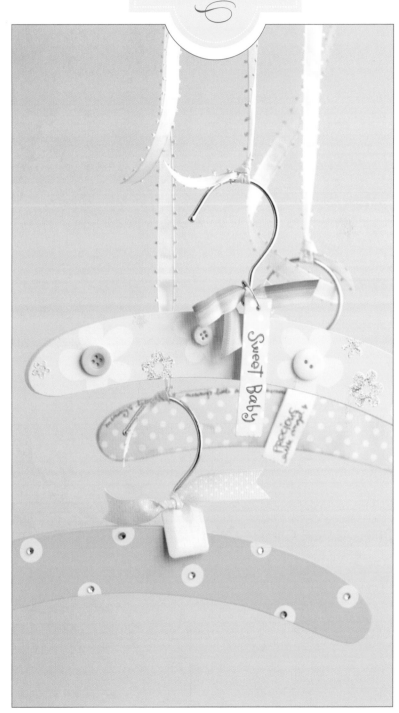

gifts for family

4

Behind every good baby, there's a good family—changing diapers, preparing bottles and giving all the love they've got to give. Don't they deserve a little something, too? From a simple gesture to a well-earned night off, discover how you can treat those in baby's life to a little babying themselves.

1 Wash and dry t-shirts

2 Slip piece of cardboard between shirt layers, preventing paint from bleeding through

3 Place shirt on hard surface and use foam brushes to apply paint to stamps

4 Test paint consistency on piece of paper before firmly stamping designs onto shirt

5 Allow to dry

Supplies: foam stamps (spring, basic shapes, misunderstood, jersey and franklin) and scrapbook colors acrylic paint (avocado, deep coral, marine, country blue, cranberry, daiquiri, chartreuse and grass stains):
Making Memories
Other: white t-shirts and silver bucket

TISSUE BOX

1 Cut paper to fit each side
2 Embellish one square with photo, stickers and ribbon
3 Attach clip with ribbon and add rub-on to outside of holder

SOAP DISPENSER

1 Cut paper to fit inside dispenser
2 Use puff paint to fill in different areas on flowers
3 While paint is still wet, sprinkle with glitter
4 Attach buttons to centers of some flowers on outside of dispenser
5 Tie ribbon and tag at top

Supplies: 5th avenue paper (elizabeth floral and die-cut), 5th avenue stickers, die-cut shapes, ribbon and colorboard stickers, rub-ons books (doodles), cheeky clips (brites) and boho chic shimmer kits (childhood and springtime): Making Memories
Tissue box and lotion bottle: Traditions Studio
Other: buttons, silver twine and puff paint

EVERYDAY BASICS
maggie holmes

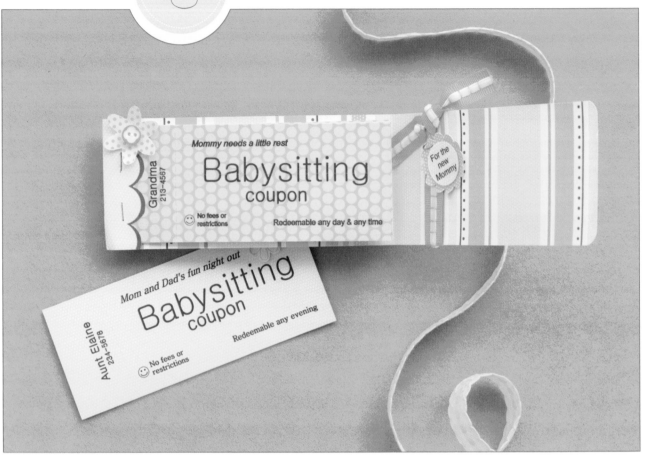

1 Print text on patterned paper, cut into long rectangles, then perforate along left side, creating coupon stub

2 Cut long strip of double-sided patterned cardstock and wrap around coupons

3 Adhere piece of deco-edged paper on left side, then fold edge over coupons and punch two staples through all layers

4 Round right two corners of long strip, fold right side over coupons and tie ribbon around front

5 Create flower tag by printing text on blue patterned paper, punch out using circle punch and adhere to orange flower sticker

6 Punch hole in top and attach to ribbon with jump ring

7 Embellish coupons with flower stickers, buttons and brads

Supplies: animal crackers paper (ella), animal crackers stickers (ella), fresh anthology button (pink), fresh anthology ribbon (coral), jump ring, mini brad and staples: Making Memories Perforating paper trimmer: Elmer's Glue Products
Thread: Coats and Clark
Font: Gulim and Arial

stitch through chipboard

1 Trace chipboard butterfly on back of purple patterned paper and cut out
2 Adhere to chipboard butterfly and machine stitch around edges
3 Create pages by tracing outside of butterfly on back of papers and cut out
4 Punch three holes down center of chipboard cover and add brads
5 Print tag text on cardstock, punch out with circle punch, add glitter chipboard circle and punch hole through both
6 Punch two holes at top of chipboard, then trace and punch corresponding holes through second chipboard butterfly and interior pages
7 Bind with metal rings and embellish

Supplies: chipboard shape (butterfly), embellishment papers (spring floral, floral egg and baby girl stripe), fresh anthology ribbon (daffodil picot), jumbo pebble brads (spring 2) and shimmer jigsaw shapes (green/purple): Making Memories
Thread: Coats and Clark, Font: Century Gothic, Other: metal binder rings

1　Paint chipboard album with scrapbook colors acrylic paint in kiwi

2　Add corrugated cardboard

3　Embellish with dimensional alpha stickers

4　Combine different papers and embellishments for inner pages

5　Leave room for pictures as well as journaling space

Supplies: fresh anthology classically defined stickers (baby), colorboard saying (baby boy), dimensional alpha stickers (baby boy), flocked chipboard mini book 6" x 9" (funky vintage), foam stamps (flowers), mini epoxy tags (baby), funky vintage paper (ruby baroque), scrapbook pad paper (baby boy), scrapbook colors acrylic paint (manila, chocolate, kiwi and cornflower), springtime button brads, classically defined (baby), metal frame combo (baby) and sweets little tags (baby): Making Memories

add three-dimensional embellishments

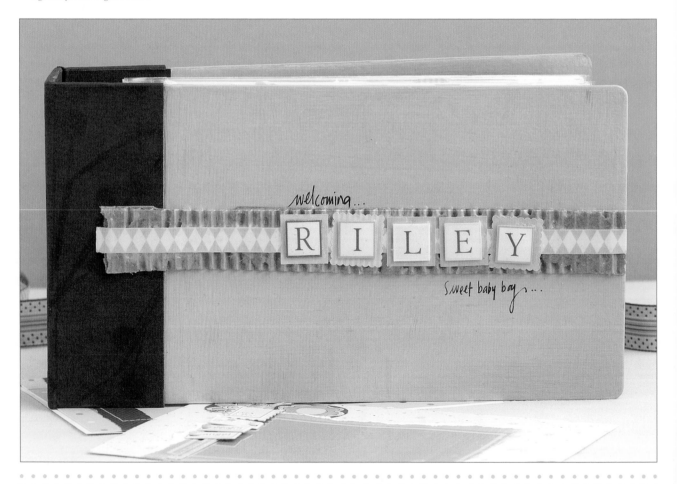

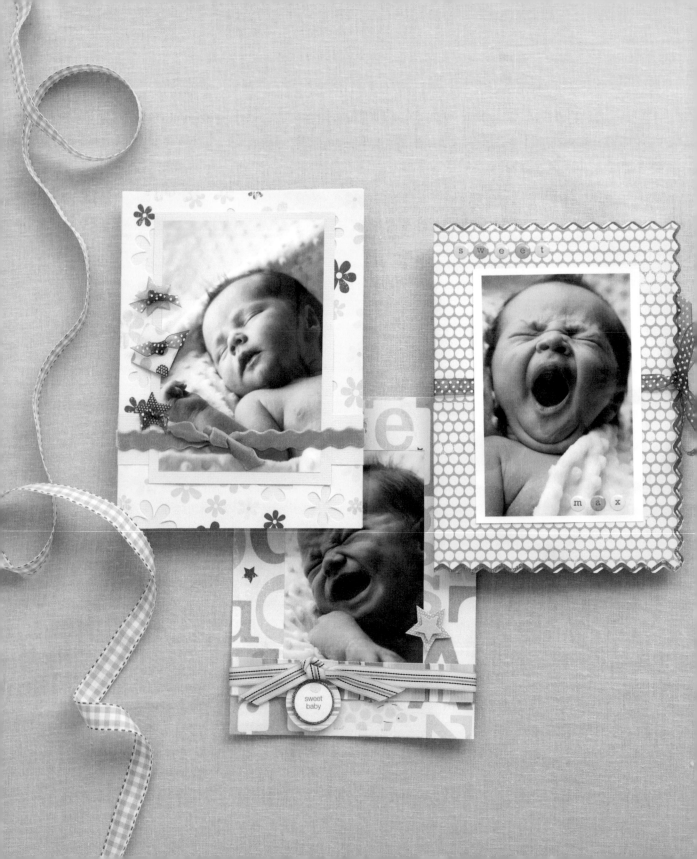

PORTFOLIO INSERTS

1 Choose paper and cut card base
2 Trim contrasting paper slightly larger than photo and adhere photo to paper
3 Place matted photo onto card base or cut an opening in card base and adhere photo behind window
4 Add trim and embellishments

Supplies: animal crackers paper and trim cards (ella and jack), animal crackers epoxy shapes, dimensional stickers and pebble stickers (jack) and animal crackers chipboard alpha: Making Memories

PORTFOLIO

1 Choose paper to house inserts and cut to be slightly larger than inserts when folded in half
2 Wrap contrasting paper and trim around middle of portfolio to secure
3 Embellish with stickers or other trims

baby

our

angel

joy

perk
at home

little
boy

It's a
Boy!

giggle

delight

BY WHOM SURRENDERED

angel

CERTIFICATE CANCELED

Ledger
Folio

No.
Certificate

No.
Shares

LEFT BY

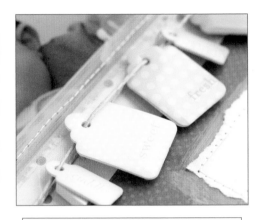

1 Make twelve 8" x 8" pages using pictures of baby
2 Add small journaling blocks to each page
3 Scan pages, and with photo editing software, add baby quotes
4 Upload pages to an online calendar printing service like Easypix
   and order copies

Supplies: blossoms jumbo (daisy and wildflower), colorboard saying (baby boy), dimensional alpha stickers (baby boy), jumbo brads (springtime), metal frame combo (baby), mini curling tags (baby), funky vintage paper (ruby baroque), noteworthy paper (esquire), scrapbook pad paper (baby boy), scrapbook colors acrylic paint (fresh anthology marine and cornflower), springtime button brads and sweets epoxy tags (baby): Making Memories Font: Zapfino, Other: string, staples and stitching

string along several epoxy tags

décor

5

When everything is new, a baby's room is a baby's world. That's why we think it should be a universe of discovery, filled with fascinating things to watch and study. Add a personalized touch to your little one's room, and watch them explore their new surroundings.

SHADOWBOXES

1 Use shadowbox back for base template and layer from there

2 Use self-adhesive sticky squares to make layers 'float'

3 Embellish with chipboard buttons, velvet brads, metal tabs and clips

CHIPBOARD ALPHABET LETTERS

1 Flip letter upside down on reverse side of paper and trace

2 Cut ⅛" inside entire letter, leaving white chipboard outline once adhered

3 Add small groupings of pictures, chipboard buttons and epoxy phrases

Supplies: animal crackers paper, stickers, buttons and epoxy phrases (jack),
noteworthy velvet brads (brown), heart pebble brads (polo), round pebble brads
(childhood), rub-ons books (alphabet 2), clips (cheeky), metal tabs
(kid expressions) and ribbon (green with blue edge): Making Memories
Ribbon: LSS

1   Print pictures on clear transparency film and trim to fit frames

2   Use protective film to sandwich photos to back of frames (or clear glue dots placed inconspicuously)

3   Rub doodles directly to front and edges of frame so picture is still visible

4   Use clear creations to add titles

5   With strong hole punch, make hanging holes in top of frames

6   String with ribbon and embellish with paper flowers

Supplies: rub-on books (doodles), baby clear creations, kids ribbons (green and blue) and baby clear frames: Making Memories
Acrylic frame: Roberts
Hole punch: Cropidile

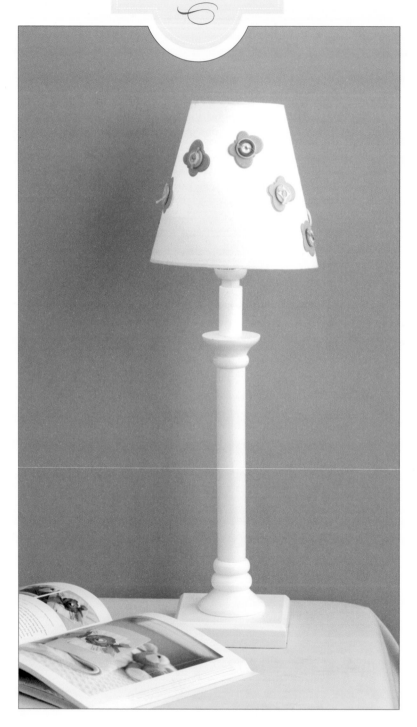

LAMPSHADE

1 With pencil, draw wavy line across shade to use as guide

2 Punch holes for grommets around shade and erase pencil line

3 Place grommets inside holes and turn shapes so butterflies appear to be flying in line

4 Set grommets and embellish centers of butterflies with buttons

NAME

1 Cover chipboard flowers with patterned paper and sand edges

2 Use cardstock to create flower centers, sew around edges and adhere to center of chipboard flowers

3 Detach knob from pre-made clothes hanger, adhere to back of chipboard flower with wood glue and allow to dry

4 Drill hole for knob in front of chipboard flower, then screw in from back and through wood

5 Spell name with shimmer jigsaw alphabet

Supplies: fresh anthology buttons, grommet shapes (butterfly), grommet tool kit, cardstock, chipboard shapes (flower), patterned papers (baby girl) and shimmer jigsaw alphabets (white):
Making Memories
Embroidery floss: DMC
Lampshade: IKEA
Wood clothes hangers (daisy shape): Michaels

1 Cut several varying flower sizes from paper

2 Add texture by crinkling and ripping random edges

3 Edge flowers with ink, glue or glitter

4 Layer several flowers on top of each other and place felt flower in center

5 Secure flowers by inserting brad

6 Hang using wall tape or small ribbon placed on back

Supplies: dimensional stickers (hillary), noteworthy embellishment
paper (artisan edge blue, stamp shape, book keeper, text, green floral
and lace flower), embellishment jar (hillary), jumbo pebble brads
(audrey), jumbo shimmer brads (ava) and shimmer kits (springtime):
Making Memories
Other: ink

1 Spray paint 4" x 6" frames white
2 Allow to dry before sanding
3 Take back out of frame, then measure and cut ledger paper to fit inside
4 Leave glass out of frame and place cards inside
5 Display on baby's dresser, shelf or wall

Supplies: dimensional stickers (ava felt and audrey glitter), noteworthy embellishment paper (artisan scalloped circle, pink floral, polka dot stripe, aqua floral and loopy stripe), embellishment jar (audrey), glitter box collections (jigsaw), jumbo pebble brads (audrey), jumbo shimmer brads (ava), noteworthy trims (ava and hillary), shimmer kits (springtime) and shimmer jigsaw alphabets (aqua): Making Memories
Other: frames and white spray paint

NAME FRAMES
christy tomlinson

add whimsy with dimensional embellishments

1 Place letters on backside of patterned papers and trace with pencil

2 Cut out each letter along traced lines and check for fit, trimming excess

3 Adhere paper cut outs to chipboard letters using spray adhesive

4 Cut additional layers of paper and use spray adhesive to attach to paper-covered letters

5 Spray letters with two to three light coats of clear varnish, allowing at least fifteen minutes between coats and three hours before handling

6 Embellish letters and hang using removable poster putty

Supplies: animal crackers paper, trim card, dimensional stickers and epoxy shapes (ella), photo décor chipboard alphabet, ribbon glue, self-healing cutting mat and universal glue: Making Memories
Craft Bond Extra Strength Spray Adhesive: Elmer's
Low Odor Clear Finish (matte): Krylon

1 Make triangle template, trace onto backside of patterned paper and cut out

2 Score each triangle ¼" from top edge and fold back

3 Glue ric-rac along back edges of each triangle

4 Glue paper triangles onto ¼" double-sided satin ribbon

5 Glue ribbon under folded edge of paper in back, then glue folded edge over ribbon

6 Make decorative knots from ribbon, glue between each triangle and embellish with buttons

Supplies: animal crackers paper (jack), bone folder, mm kids ric-rac trim (sam), shimmer alphas (teal) and fresh anthology buttons: Making Memories

use ric-rac as a decorative edge

BIRD MOBILE

1 Paint chipboard flower and add shimmer
2 Cut bird shapes from paper, stuff with batting and stitch around edges
3 Add grommet to chipboard
4 Use wire to attach and hang birds from chipboard
5 Cover wire with pink ribbons
6 Add feathers

DRAGONFLY MOBILE

1 Cut out dragonflies and draw in details on front
2 Paint chipboard flower and add pictures and letters
3 Add dragonflies with pop dots
4 Add grommet and ribbon for hanging

Supplies: scrapbook pad paper (baby girl), grommets (pink flower and green), 8" chipboard flowers, shimmer (boho chic pink), scrapbook colors acrylic paint (tulip, pea pod and robin's egg) and shimmer stickers (pink lemonade): Making Memories
Ribbon: Wal-Mart
Tombow pen: Grey
Other: wire, batting, feathers and pop dots

attach sheer frame and embellishments

1   Print two photos and insert into clip frames
2   Cut green paper to fit behind glass of center frame
3   Attach paper strip and name label and secure glass with clips
4   Attach sheer frame embellishments and button to front of glass
5   Cut ribbon to desired length and attach to backs of frames
6   Attach eyelet to top of ribbon for hanging
7   Hide eyelet by folding over ribbon and attach button

Supplies: 8" x 8" scrapbook pad paper (baby boy), colorboard sayings (baby boy), noteworthy paper, funky vintage trims (lizzie) and sheer frame combo (baby): Making Memories
Buttons: Melissa Frances
Clip frames: IKEA

1 Set printer to correct setting and print picture onto transparency
2 Make shadowbox background by using patterned paper and letter stickers
3 Add gravel and assemble shadowbox
4 Handle carefully, as gravel will damage picture

Supplies: dimensional alpha stickers and scrapbook pad paper (baby boy):
Making Memories
Shadowbox and gravel: IKEA
Other: transparencies

raise letters from border surface

1 Paint wood pieces (have hardware store cut and drill holes)

2 Stamp and tie wood pieces together

3 Add stickers

Supplies: dimensional alpha stickers (baby girl), scrapbook
colors acrylic paint (spotlight and celery) and vintage hip ribbon:
Making Memories
Dot stamp: Amuse

add embellishments to chipboard

1 Paint chipboard pieces and stamp
2 Apply glitter to chipboard and add embellishments

Supplies: fresh anthology button and jigsaw shapes,
jumbo blossoms, 8" chipboard shapes (spring/easter),
scrapbook pad colorboards (baby girl), vintage hip
ribbon and simply fabulous gem stickers:
Making Memories
Bling circle: Heidi Swapp

create a complimentary collage

1 Use patterned papers, embellishments and photos to decorate plain chipboard rectangles

2 Align rectangles in order and punch holes on top and bottom of each card

3 Punch holes and weave ribbon through chipboard, starting from bottom of left side to top and back down right side

Supplies: mini colorboard stickers (baby boy and baby girl), deck the halls paper (diagonal stripe), funky vintage (lizzie polka dot paisley and scallop stripe), travel journal, shimmer jigsaw alphabet (white) and shimmer jigsaw shapes (hearts and stars): Making Memories
Ribbon: Michaels
Chipboard rectangles: Maya Road

1 Randomly place alphabet stickers on photo matte,
   filling all white space
2 Use craft knife to trim any stickers from edges
3 Place matte in frame and add photo

Supplies: funky vintage flocked alphabet stickers (lizzie):
Making Memories
Frame: IKEA

moments & memories

6

It may not seem like it when it's three in the morning and you're trying to soothe a screaming child, but believe it or not, a baby's first year goes by pretty quickly. After that, it's just a memory. So how do you make sure you don't forget a thing? Make a record of it. The big, the small and the in-between.

STITCHED GRID

1 Cut paper to fit back of shadowbox
2 Cut rectangle from brown cardstock and page protector
3 Lay page protector on top of cardstock and stitch grid onto both
4 Cut slits at top of each square and slide photo into each pocket
   (be careful to only cut through page protector and not through cardstock)
5 Embellish pocket fronts with numbers, frames and rub-ons
6 Embellish shadowbox bottom with baby name, paper and flowers

MAGNETIC BOARD

1 Paint board and allow to dry
2 Adhere paper to board
3 Cut stems for flowers from paper and adhere to board
4 Adhere flowers, rub-ons and buttons
5 Use magnetic clip to hang photo

Supplies: shimmer alphabet stickers (silver), cheeky jigsaw (circle lowercase plain), sheer frame combo (baby), metal frame combo (love), fresh anthology embellishment paper (eliza), rub-on books (doodles, flourishes and icons), jumbo blossoms (wildflower and spotlight), packaging tape (collection 2 and school days), scrapbook colors acrylic paint (strawberries and cream and funky vintage seafoam), rub-on alphabets (trademark small white), noteworthy paper, jumbo pebble brads (pink and brown), fresh anthology metal index tabs (girl), funky vintage fabulous flowers (lizzie), scrapbook colors acrylic paint, mm kids paper (bella), modular organization system panels (brushed silver) and modular organization system accessories (bulldog clips): Making Memories
Rub-on birds: Hambly Screen Prints
Other: shadowbox and buttons

embellish tops of interior cards

1 Remove all hardware, old papers or cloth, and use sandpaper to roughen up surface of box

2 Coat with primer, let dry, then paint with desired color and let dry

3 Cut assorted papers to fit box inside and out

4 Using PVA glue, paste papers to box and let dry

5 Using sandpaper and other materials, distress box and clean dust off with damp towel

6 Reinstall hardware

7 Use decorative tags to add baby name to box

Supplies: paper pad (baby girl), dimensional stickers (baby girl), pebble brads (brown and pink), shimmer jigsaw (pink and white), pink blossoms, sweets tags (baby) and metal index tabs: Making Memories
Distress ink: Tim Holz
Other: PVA glue, spray paint and sandpaper

attach simple embellishment to card

1   Cut cardstock to fit cube
2   Stamp image onto cut cardstock
3   Glue cardstock to cube
4   Add photograph, chipboard, flowers and rhinestones

Supplies: jumbo blossoms, simply fabulous gem stickers
and colorboards (baby girl): Making Memories
Dot stamp: Amuse
Cardstock: Bazzill

thread ribbon through grommet

1 Paint chipboard

2 Punch holes for grommets and ribbon

3 Add grommets and ribbon

4 Add photo to frames and adhere to chipboard

5 Add sticker

Supplies: grommet shapes (flower), funky vintage trims (ruby), fresh anthology metal frame combos (love), vintage hip frames (dot), colorboard sayings (baby girl) and dimensional stickers (baby girl): Making Memories

add monochromatic depth

1 Trim chipboard pieces to 7" x 10"
2 Cover chipboard with patterned paper
3 Drill ⅛" hole ½" from top, side and
   bottom (each piece will have four holes)
4 Trim ledger paper in various shapes, outline
   with pen and add month at top with rub-ons
   or computer font
5 Adhere photos
6 Embellish chipboard pieces with ribbon, stickers
   and buttons
7 Attach chipboard pieces with ribbon

Supplies: noteworthy paper (audrey die-cut scallop,
ava die-cut ledger, audrey pink floral, audrey polka dot
stripe, ava loopy stripe, ava aqua floral and hillary green
floral), ledger paper (bookkeeper, esquire and text),
dimensional flower stickers (audrey), chipboard alphabet
(audrey), embellishment jar (audrey), heart brad, cheeky
silver clip and noteworthy trims (ava):
Making Memories
Other: chipboard

scrapbooking

7

Scrapbooking is something we all know and love. But when it comes to your baby, the term doesn't seem to fit. Think of all the things you'll be remembering. Footprints and footsteps. First smiles and first words. These things aren't scraps. They're once-in-a-lifetime treasures.

CORA
wendy bretz

1. Adhere ric-rac ledger to cardstock
2. Create various sized circles with punch and place around paper
3. Adhere lace trim and jumbo shimmer brads
4. Adhere dimensional stickers and title
5. Attach photo

Supplies: noteworthy scalloped circle (audrey), noteworthy aqua floral (ava), noteworthy loopy stripe (ava), noteworthy ric-rac ledger, noteworthy trims (hillary), noteworthy dimensional felt stickers (ava), noteworthy jumbo shimmer brads and simply fabulous velvet alpha sticker: Making Memories
Cardstock: Bazzill

1 Use spring foam stamps and paint to create several colors and sizes of butterflies on transparencies

2 Apply glitter to butterflies while paint is still wet, allow to dry and cut out

3 Use ledger paper as background, then adhere layers of patterned papers

4 Place pictures on layout and adhere stickers, overlapping main picture

5 Place pins in butterflies, fold upwards and use glue dots to attach to page

6 Place shimmer brads around circle die-cut and place title on page

7 Staple ribbons to page and make random stitches across layout

Supplies: classically defined (fresh anthology memories), fresh anthology trim card (eliza), noteworthy paper (audrey pink floral, die-cut scalloped circle and polka dot stripe, ava aqua floral and hillary ric-rac ledger die-cut), scrapbook colors acrylic paint (lipstick and sea foam), scrapbook shimmer kits (springtime), shimmer brads (valentine love), shimmer jigsaw alphabets (aqua), simply fabulous velvet alpha (aqua ice), spring foam stamps and vintage hip trinkets: Making Memories

layer petite embellishments

1 Adhere patterned paper to cardstock
2 Stamp journaling and cut
3 Punch holes and add brads to clears shapes
4 Add photos and journaling strips
5 Add ribbon, flower and pin

Supplies: noteworthy scallop ledger (audrey), funky vintage fabulous flower (lizzie), brads (buttons), fresh anthology classically defined (baby), magnetic stamps (providence and expressions), vintage hip trinkets pins and funky vintage clears (white tags and shapes): Making Memories

1 Stamp journaling onto cardstock and cut into strips
2 Add photos, stickers and journal strips to patterned paper
3 Stamp accents onto layout

Supplies: noteworthy artisan edge blue (hillary), magnetic stamps
(providence and ornaments), clear creations (doodles) and classically
defined (baby): Making Memories

TAGGED
leah fung

1 Punch decorative border along top of brown patterned paper, layer over three other patterned papers and machine stitch

2 Adhere photo to page

3 Print on tag, add string, adhere to page, machine stitch and add letter sticker

4 Print on mini tag, tie onto chipboard letter and adhere to upper left corner of photo

5 Adhere threaded button

6 Using tag curling tool, gently attach two metal tags to top of page

Supplies: curling tags (baby), tag curler tool, travel journaling tag, travel papers (stripe, diamond brocade and journal), travel printed jigsaw alpha chipboards and travel stamp alpha sticker: Making Memories
Font: Arial, Button: Joanns, Punch: Fiskars, Thread: Coats and Clark

gently attach metal tags

use grommet words as embellishments

1 Cut plain sheet of paper to 6⅜" x 9½"

2 Cut different patterned papers into twelve 2⅜" x 2⅛" squares, adhere to plain sheet of paper and machine stitch

3 Adhere quilted sheet to cover of album and buff corners of paper with sanding block

4 Using glue dots or foam tape, adhere embellishments to each square of quilted cover

5 Tie different ribbons around spine of album

6 For interior page, adhere and machine stitch patterned papers and embellish

Supplies: animal crackers paper (jack), stickers and tags, button brads (springtime), fresh anthology ribbon (avocado scallop and daffodil picot), funky vintage flocked mini book (chartreuse), grommet words (baby), mm kids trims, sanding block, sweets (baby springtime and hearts) and woven ribbon (red and white): Making Memories
Font: Batang, Buttons: Joanns, Thread: Coats and Clark

MIRACLE
maggie holmes

1 Print photos and attach to page
2 Cut strips of packaging tape and paper and attach to left of photos
3 Apply ready-to-glitter stickers to page and add glitter
4 Embellish with clears tags and shapes, rub-ons and stickers
5 Write journaling with brown marker

Supplies: noteworthy artisan edge blue (hillary), scrapbook pad paper (baby boy), colorboard sayings (baby boy), clears tags and shapes (funky vintage), packaging tape (boho chic), shimmer kit (boho chic), brads (circle cityscape), ready-to-glitter stickers (alpha large), shimmer jigsaw shapes (hearts and stars), rub-on books (flourishes and icons) and brad value pack (stars): Making Memories
Marker: ZIG

overlap embellishments for depth

1. Attach envelopes to layout
2. Create title with clears alphabet
3. Attach strips of ribbon to left of title
4. Paint chipboard shape and adhere to left of title
5. Embellish page with stickers, brads and rub-ons
6. Use marker to write the contents on each envelope

Supplies: noteworthy stamp (hillary), rub-on books (flourishes and icons), funky vintage flocked labels and ephemera stickers (lizzie), noteworthy ribbon, classically defined (baby and family and friends), fresh anthology (velvet brads), fresh anthology (jigsaw plain), funky vintage trims (lizzie), funky vintage clears alphabet (chocolate and lizzie), clears tags and shapes (funky vintage) and scrapbook color effects (metallic): Making Memories
Marker: ZIG, Other: envelopes

REMEMBER
maggie holmes

1 Cut two strips from orange paper, cutting one side of each with deco scissors

2 Adhere patterned papers to pink cardstock and machine stitch

3 Adhere photo, journaling, mini clips and tag to page

4 Cut out large numbers, machine stitch around edges, add sequins and attach using foam tape

5 Print script text on blue patterned paper, cut out and adhere to large numbers and tag

6 Adhere pink trim to top of page and staple ends

Supplies: animal crackers paper (ella and jack), cheeky flat clips (neutral), cheeky ribbon (gathered grosgrain pink) and jumbo pebble brad (fresh anthology): Making Memories
Font: Century Gothic and Suzanne Quill
Cardstock: Bazzill
Sequins: Westrim Crafts
Thread: Coats and Clark

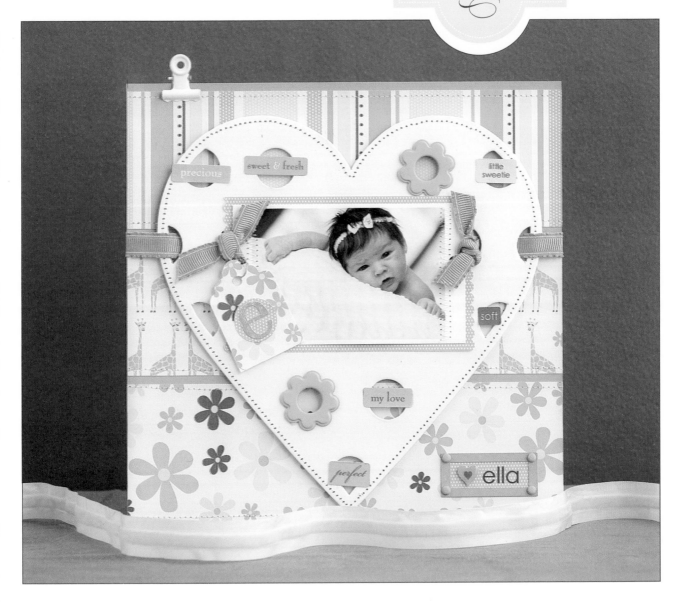

1 Adhere and machine stitch patterned papers to orange cardstock

2 Machine stitch around edge of heart chipboard

3 Double matte photo, cut edge of orange patterned paper with deco scissors and machine stitch on right edge of photo

4 Punch holes on left and right side of matted photo, thread through ribbon and tie

5 Put adhesive on back of chipboard and adhere to page

6 Add embellishments

Supplies: animal crackers paper (ella), animal crackers pebble stickers (ella), fresh anthology alpha sticker (eliza), grommets (flowers), label holder, mini brads, sweets (heart) 8" chipboard heart and trim: Making Memories
Font: Suzanne Quill and Century Gothic
Thread: Coats and Clark

ALEX LEONARD A DAY AT THE BEACH ALMOST DONE WITH PHOTO TAKING BEING SUPER SILLY BUT SO GOSH DERN CUTE HUH? AUGUST 2007.

stack details for interest

1 Use 12" x 12" background as base, adding 7" x 4" strip of green cardstock
   in lower left corner
2 Adhere green paper dots on top of strip, placing black brads in center of each
3 Cut 1" strips of black patterned paper and mount to right of photo,
   pop dotting each ½" apart
4 Print and place journaling above brown striped and black paper
5 Add embellishments

Supplies: 5th avenue paper and colorboard (sophia) and white mini brads:
Making Memories
Font: Bensgothic

1 Place three 4" x 6" photos at top of page

2 Print date on white cardstock with black text box and adhere under photos

3 Place patterned paper inside metal-rimmed tags and mount beside die-cut flowers with shimmer brads

4 Place 'play' text on middle of cream cardstock, adding black scroll icon underneath and chipboard on either side

5 Adhere metal charm at bottom right of page

Supplies: 5th avenue paper (elizabeth and sophia), jumbo shimmer brads (noteworthy), large metal rims, tagmaker, 5th avenue trim card and chipboard alpha (sophia) and charmed enamel: Making Memories

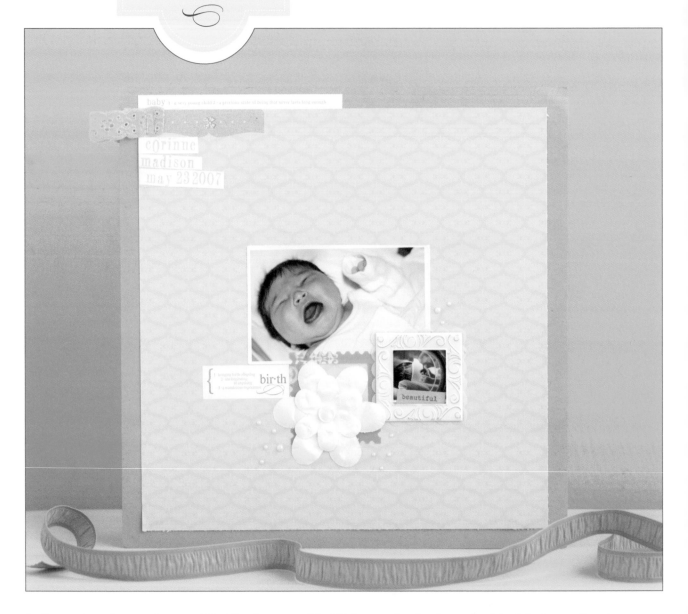

1 Cut one sheet of patterned paper to 11" x 11" and mount on 12" x 12" sheet
2 Add photos, frames, flower, stickers and pearls
3 Stamp journaling strips and add to page
4 Add ribbon

Supplies: clear creations baby, funky vintage scallop stripe paper, classically defined stickers (baby), funky clears tags and shapes (white frames), jumbo blossoms, kraft emphemera stickers, simply fabulous gem stickers (pearls) and trim card (easter): Making Memories

1 Cut one sheet of patterned paper to 11" x 11" and mount onto 12" x 12" sheet
2 Layer tags in center of page
3 Add photo with transparency
4 Cut and add scallop strip
5 Add flowers, stickers and stamped journaling strips

Supplies: clear creations baby, general travel paper (diamond brocade), tropical travel paper (hibiscus), classically defined stickers (baby), funky vintage fabulous flowers, kraft ephemera stickers, simply fabulous gem stickers and dyed tags (fresh anthology): Making Memories

1 Print 4" x 9" photo and place on bottom of page, printing title onto photo
2 Rub crown on white paper, place in center of chipboard frame and adhere to right of photo
3 Trim patterned paper into large half circles and layer above photo
4 Print journaling onto brown striped cardstock and place along right side of photo

Supplies: noteworthy paper (light pink), funky vintage patterned paper (lizzie), rub-on flourishes and icons book (brown crown), funky vintage tags and frames (pink parenthesis), funky vintage ribbon (lizzie), chipboard heart and brown frame (cheeky jigsaw), and letter 'a' chipboard (audrey): Making Memories
Font: Jailberd Jenna
Daily something brush: Ali Edwards

combine bold color accents

1 Print 9" x 6" photo and place in center of page
2 Trim velvet sayings sheets and place onto left of page, directly under photo
3 Print journaling in pink on dark brown cardstock and place under photo on right
4 Rub white flourish directly over bottom numbers
5 Embellish with half circle and ribbon on left and glittery chipboard on right

Supplies: velvet sayings (baby), funky vintage paper (lizzie), funky vintage ribbon
and button (lizzie), like it is stickers and rub-on book (flourishes and icons):
Making Memories
Font: Jailberd Jenna
Chipboard star: Technique Tuesday

mix textures and materials

1 Cut ledger patterned paper, creating smaller sheet, and piece together

2 Sew along seams, hiding line

3 Adhere floral paper and add title using chipboard alpha stickers

4 Add rub-on title and shimmer brads

5 Attach small silver grommet, photo and dimensional sticker

Supplies: noteworthy scallop ledger (audrey), noteworthy green floral (hillary), jumbo shimmer brads (noteworthy), dimensional glitter stickers (noteworthy), noteworthy chipboard alphabet stickers (audrey), grommet tool and rub-on books (alphabet 2): Making Memories
Cardstock: Bazzill

1   Cut artisan edge patterned paper, creating smaller sheet, and piece together

2   Cut strip of green floral paper, adhere to layout and attach trim with staples

3   Using glitter die-cuts, create circle embellishments with circle punch and
    adhere to top and bottom of layout

4   Place title along side of ribbon and attach photo

Supplies: noteworthy papers (artisan edge blue, hillary green floral and loopy stripe ava),
noteworthy trim card (hillary), noteworthy glitter die-cuts, noteworthy pebble clips (hillary)
and noteworthy chipboard alphabet stickers (audrey): Making Memories
Cardstock: Bazzill

first celebrations

8

Being a baby can be hard work. They're constantly experimenting and learning, until rolling over turns to crawling, and crawling turns to walking, and babbling turns to speaking. And that's just the beginning. That's why your baby's first celebrations are so important. It gives them the chance to catch their breath and learn how to party.

INVITATION

1 Create invitation on computer and print

2 Matte with red paper and cut into nine equal squares

3 Place squares into small zip-top bag

4 Cut rectangle of polka dot paper, fold over top of bag and staple

5 Punch circle from orange paper and smaller circle from notebook paper and adhere

6 Stamp 'you're invited' onto notebook paper circle

PARTY HAT

1 Form red patterned paper into cone shape and secure

2 Punch different sized circles from paper and adhere to hat

3 Attach number sticker and ribbon to hat

FAVOR

1 Line box with paper and secure with adhesive

2 Punch circle from paper, add star tag with brad and attach to front of box

3 Tie ribbon to box handle

Supplies (both pages): cheeky trims (emery), tag maker punch (circle medium and circle large), felt ribbon (holiday), rub-on books (flourishes and icons), brad value pack (circle black and white and silver), cheeky paper (emery), mm kids paper (max), jumbo brads (springtime, childhood and black and white), nothing but numbers stickers (spotlight), tagged vellum star, textured tape (cheeky emery) and magnetic stamps (all occasion): Making Memories
Label sticker: Martha Stewart Crafts
Dye Ink Pad: Memories
Font: American Typewriter

LAYOUT

1 Print photo and mount onto white cardstock
2 Create border with marker and ruler
3 Cut photo into nine equal squares
4 Adhere squares onto red paper, leaving small gap between each
   and attach to layout
5 Layer ribbon and textured tape at bottom of layout
6 Stamp birthday sayings onto tag and embellish

FAVOR CUPS

1 Cut assorted patterned papers to 2" x 10"

2 Trim 8 oz. white paper cups to stand 2½" tall

3 Wrap patterned papers around cups, leaving edges uneven and secure with double-sided tape

4 Decorate with stickers, line with tissue paper and fill with candies or party favors

PARTY HAT

1 Cut 12" circle from patterned paper, cut in half, form cones and secure with double-sided tape or staples

2 Punch one hole on either side of hat and add ribbon

3 Add personalized embellishments

CUPCAKE TOPPERS

1 Cut embellishment from patterned papers with die-cut machine or use stickers

2 With PVA glue, attach embellishment to tip of toothpick, let dry and place in frosted cupcake top

Supplies (both pages): animal crackers paper and stickers (ella): Making Memories
Other: colorfast seam binding, thread, assorted hand-made embellishments, double-sided tape, 8 oz. white paper cups, assorted tissue paper, PVA glue, toothpicks, spray paint, sandpaper and old box
Distress Ink: Tim Holtz

KEEPSAKE TREASURE BOX

1 Remove all hardware, papers or cloth and use sandpaper
   to roughen surface of box
2 Coat with primer, dry, then paint with desired color and let dry
3 Cut assorted papers to fit box and adhere using PVA glue paste
4 Use distressing materials to distress box and clean dust with cloth
5 Re-install hardware and add baby's name to box with tag

FESTIVE FLAGS

1 Cut assorted 4" x 6" triangles, making sure point is in the middle
2 Adhere two flags together, trim with pinking shears and stitch along edge
3 Sew completed flags to ribbon

stack a variety of themed word fetti

1 Draw four intersecting lines vertically and horizontally across top and left-hand side of white cardstock

2 Add title and clear brackets to top line just created

3 Punch 1½" circle of orange patterned paper, attach circle and clear circle embellishment using silver brad and staple bottom corner of circle

4 Add halloween word fetti, ribbons and stars

5 Cut small strip of patterned paper and align with flocking sheet along left side of photo

6 Print 4" x 6" photo, matte with black cardstock and adhere to layout under title

7 Create subtitle on computer and attach to top of photo

Supplies: halloween paper (orange and word), flocking and foiling kit, velvet stickers, clear shapes (funky vintage), shimmer brads, chipboard buttons and trims (halloween): Making Memories
Cardstock: Bazzill, Pigma Pen (black): Sakura
Font: Two Peas In A Bucket (airplanes), Other: staples

1 Trim patterned paper to 8½" x 11"

2 Add white cardstock and stitch around border

3 Matte photo with orange patterned paper and adhere to layout

4 Attach clear photo corner, brads, frame and letter 'h'

5 Create journaling strips on computer and attach

6 Hand cut computer title and adhere

Supplies: halloween paper (newsprint and orange), black shimmer jigsaw, mini brad value pack (bats), clears shapes (funky vintage) and orange frame (halloween): Making Memories
Cardstock: Bazzill, Font: Fling
Other: stitching

1 Have plexiglas cut at a local glass shop or cut using band saw

2 Drill holes in top of each piece

3 Cut papers from each page and adhere to each plexiglas piece

4 Use halloween embellishments to decorate pages after pictures have been placed

5 Use book rings to hold plexiglas pieces together

Supplies: cardstock tags and flocked ephemera (halloween), halloween paper (funky stripe and foiled black on black), pebble brads (black and white) and trim card (valentine love 2): Making Memories
Graph overlay: Hambly Screen Prints
Notecard: www.everyjotandtitle.com
Other: crochet trims (scarlet lime) and plexiglas

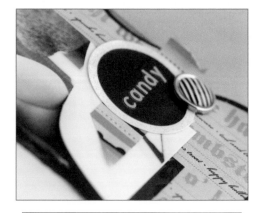

layer paper and embellishments to create texture

1 Cut out artisan design from back of striped paper and adhere to overlay

2 Cut black paper and adhere on top

3 Place photo over black paper

4 Write on notecard and place onto page, overlapping picture

5 Use halloween embellishments to decorate page

6 Staple ribbon and trims to layout

Supplies: cardstock tags, colorboard too, flocked ephemera, velvet stickers and word fetti stickers (halloween), halloween paper (funky stripe, foiled black on black, large dot, word pattern and flocked spider web), pebble brads (black and white) and alpha/border stickers and ephemera stickers (halloween page kit):
Making Memories
Other: plexiglas

We fit your first **CHRISTMAS** in between naps. There was no way we could get through all **those presents** in one sitting. You spent the **ENTIRE DAY** putting things in your mouth. You could have cared less about the presents themselves!

•*always*

ALLA.8months.HOLIDAY**05**

make the holidays glitter

1   Print journaling onto green cardstock and adhere to patterned paper

2   Paint chipboard circles, cut in half with scissors and use as page divider

3   Place chipboard inside photo frame and decorate with glitter, ribbon and clear sticker

Supplies: st. nick paper (flocked and green dot), vintage hip frames (dot), metal embellishment (circle), clearly defined stickers, velvet sayings (wedding) and simply fabulous gem brads (maddi): Making Memories
Font: Zurich Bold
Other: kraft and white cardstock and glitter

1 Print date and journaling onto cardstock and adhere to paper
2 Paint chipboard stars, place onto metal rimmed tags and decorate
   with mini brads
3 Place sticker frame over photo
4 Decorate with metal frame and sticker

Supplies: metal frame combo (winter), chipboard game shapes
(stars), mini colorboard stickers (merry christmas), metal rimmed
tags (white) and velvet sayings (family): Making Memories
Fonts: Courier New and Impact
Other: white cardstock

CANDY CANE
nia reddy

1 Cut red script paper to 3" x 5½", trimming one edge with large scalloped scissors, and adhere paper, photo and tag as shown

2 Cut holly paper to 2½" x 4", rounding top left corner and adhere over tag

3 Add letter, scroll stickers, large striped strip and ephemera sticker

4 Cut holly leaf shape from patterned paper, score along center and add buttons

5 Adhere small piece from holiday collage paper and add metal embellishment and journaling

Supplies: christmas paper (stripes, hollyberry,newsprint), christmas alpha stickers, ledger ric-rac paper (noteworthy) and metal frame combos (christmas): Making Memories
Other: red buttons, large tag and scalloped scissors

1 Adhere small frame to top of paisley metal frame, punch two holes in top, string through ribbon and tie

2 Cut four holly leaf shapes from paisley dot paper, score along center and add buttons for holly berries

3 Adhere title to frame and ephemera sticker to takeout box

Supplies: charmed frame (beaded), paisley dot paper, holiday ephemera stickers and vintage hip paisley frame: Making Memories
Other: takeout box, red buttons and ribbon

thank you cards

9

Maybe it's their smiles. Maybe it's their bald heads. Maybe it's their effervescent personalities. But for some reason babies make friends fast. Which is great, because from the parent's perspective, help is always welcome. So how do you thank all of the people who have been a friend to both you and your baby? With style.

thank you

(ba·by)

ba·by

1 · a very young child;
an infant
2 · pure sweetness
3 · the end-all, be-all of cute

Thank You

thank
you

add sticker sentiments

SWEET THANK YOU

1 Stamp images on tag
2 Add ribbon to tag
3 Stamp images and thank you onto card
4 Add tag and sticker

THANK YOU

1 Cut cardstock and round corners
2 Add paint to edges of cardstock and stamp
3 Apply sticker and rub-on
4 Punch hole, then add ribbon and flower
5 Add stick pin

Supplies: magnetic stamps (providence and ornaments), funky vintage trims (ruby), scrapbook pad tag (baby boy), colorboard sayings (boy), blossoms (rose petal), crystal brads (clear), trim cards (easter), kraft ephemera and vintage hip trinkets: Making Memories
Circle stamps: Autumn Leaves

POCKET TOTE

1 Cut rectangle shape from transparency, punch half circle at top and adhere corners of transparency onto patterned paper with clear adhesive

2 Machine stitch edges of transparency on three straight-edge sides

3 Wrap small rectangular box using sheet with stitched transparency (if desired, use additional sheet of patterned paper to wrap around back of box and adhere to first sheet)

4 Fold down and tape papers on one end of box and slide papers off box

5 Cut 1½" x 10" strip of patterned paper, fold three times lengthwise for a thicker ½" strip and adhere last fold in place

6 Tape ends of strip inside newly created bag for handle

7 Adhere strip of striped paper along lower front of bag, adhere ribbon around bag and tie smaller piece of same ribbon on front

CARD INSERT

1 Print journaling within pink-lined box on cardstock and fold in half

2 Adhere two blossoms and threaded button using glue dots

Supplies: animal crackers paper (ella), blossoms (wildflower peach), fresh anthology button and fresh anthology ribbon (cantaloupe floral scallop): Making Memories
Cardstock: Bazzill Basics
Circle Punch: Marvy Uchida
Thread: Coats and Clark
Transparency: Office Depot
Fonts: SuzanneQuill SH and CopperplGoth BT

thank you
so much
for your
thoughtful
gift for
our baby

You are Kind
Generous
Thoughtful
Surprising
and Caring
Thanks, friend!

thank
you

Christy

layer embellishments over paper edge

1 Cut and fold pink cardstock and adhere baby-themed journaling sheet to front

2 Cut strip of white cardstock and punch notebook edge along strip

3 Adhere and machine stitch white strip to top of journaling sheet

4 Place mini button brads in epoxy flowers

5 Adhere epoxy flowers, epoxy heart and bookplate to cards using glue dots

Supplies: animal crackers journaling book (ella), mini button brads,
mini flower brads and sweets (flowers and heart): Making Memories
Cardstock: Bazzill Basics
Notebook Edge Punch: Stampin' Up
Thread: Coats and Clark
Fonts: Century Gothic (lion card), Times New Roman (alligator card)
and Garamond (hippo card)

combine different textures for visual interest

1   Cut rectangles of noteworthy paper
2   Mount onto brown cardstock
3   Rub tiny amount of brown paint onto metal word fetti
4   Embellish each card with ribbon, rub-ons and more

Supplies: noteworthy paper, textured tape (baby boy and baby girl), colorboard sayings (baby girl), fresh anthology trims (eliza), clears shapes and frames, scrapbook colors acrylic paint (chocolate), brads (circle cityscape), mm kids trims (kate), embellishment paper (cosmopolitan collection), jumbo blossoms (wildflower and spotlight) and metal word fetti (card sayings): Making Memories

1 Trace shapes onto patterned paper and cut out

2 Use marker to outline shapes

3 Stamp 'thanks' onto each card

4 Stamp flourish images onto each card

5 Embellish with gem stickers

Supplies: 8" x 8" scrapbook pad (baby girl and baby boy),
gem stickers (maddi) and magnetic stamps (ornaments and
all occasion): Making Memories
Marker: ZIG
Ink pad: Memories

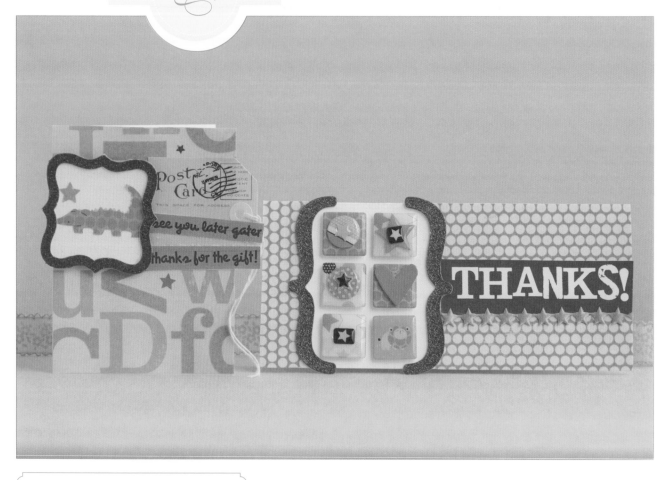

layer shapes to create a three-dimensional accent

ALLIGATOR

1   Place alligator sticker in center of white cardstock and surround with noteworthy shimmer chipboard

2   Print text on green cardstock, cut into strips and place on mini tag

THANKS!

1   Mount shimmer chipboard shapes on either side of 1" piece of white cardstock

2   Mount epoxy shapes in open center, layering with chipboard pieces

Supplies (both pages): animal crackers paper, epoxy shapes and trim card (jack), gameboard shapes (hearts), travel journaling tag, animal crackers paper and epoxy shapes (ella), tropical travel paper, shimmer jigsaw flowers, woven labels and silver brads: Making Memories

combine glitter, gemstone and epoxy

THANK YOU

1 Place flowers on pop dots, adding small velvet brad and mini jewel in center of each

2 Place white velvet letters on white cardstock

3 Adhere fabric saying to bottom left of card

SO VERY MUCH

1 Print journaling on brown cardstock and adhere to left center of card

2 Layer noteworthy shimmer chipboard flowers, placing velvet brad and jewel in center of each

3 Adhere to double layered circle and place to right of card

attach message tag with decorative brad

RECYCLED SCRAPS

1 Trim paper scraps slightly smaller than card face (use more of one pattern)
2 Adhere trimmed scraps to card front with double-sided tape or glue stick
3 Glue trim to cover paper seams
4 Add 'thank you' rub-on to bottom of card

PHOTO CARDS

1 Using computer, crop digital photo to measure 4" x 3¾"
2 Print photo onto medium weight cardstock and trim card to measure 4" x 5½"
3 Cut piece of patterned paper with deco scissors and adhere to card
4 Glue ribbon to top edge of decorative paper and add rub-on

Supplies (both pages): fresh anthology paper (eliza and sydney), fresh anthology trim card (eliza), spring trim card, jumbo pebble brads (springtime), thank you rub-ons and mm kids trim (ethan and bella): Making Memories
Grosgrain ribbon: Michaels
Incredi-tape: Coffee Break Design
Deco scissors: EK Success

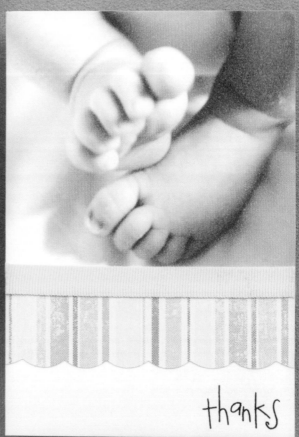

PHOTO TAGS

suzonne stirling

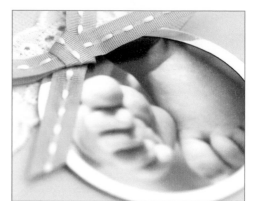

photo details can personalize your project

PHOTO RIMS

1 Embellish blank A2 size card with paper scrap that measures slightly
   smaller than front of card
2 Glue ribbon over paper seam
3 Print small photos onto photo paper and cut out tag of desired size
4 Place photo inside tag rim and use tag maker to crimp edges
5 Add rub-on to bottom of card

THANK YOU

1 Embellish blank A2 size card with paper scrap that measures
   slightly smaller than front of card

2 Glue ribbon over paper seam

3 Add rub-on to bottom of card

Supplies (both pages): mm kids paper (ethan), fresh anthology trim
card (sydney), ribbon cards (rose petal and mango), thank you rub-ons,
tag maker (large circle rims) and animal crackers paper (jack):
Making Memories
Incredi-tape: Coffee Break Design

book end

10

keisha campbell
beijing, china

Keisha gathers her inspiration from many places, including magazines, books and, of course, her own creative brainstorming. But even then, there's no exact plan. She enjoys starting with something that she loves (like a new photo) and then lets nature take its course. Because she and her family live in Beijing, she finds most of her unique crafting supplies online.

leah fung
san diego, california

Leah Fung makes decent use of both the left and right sides of her brain. This Medicinal Chemist, chess strategist, Japanese anime-lover and mother of two is both pragmatic and silly. Sounds like the perfect combination to us. As you probably guessed, her scrapbooking style is equally hard to categorize, but she does profess a love for clean lines, metal embellishments and sewing.

wilna furstenberg
prince albert, canada

Wilna was born and raised in South Africa, where she earned her degree in fine arts and met her husband of 15 years. She and her family have now lived in Canada for two years, where her husband practices medicine and their three girls practice ballet. Besides her love of family, friends and scrapbooking, Wilna likes to cook and share a good meal.

jill godon
ontario, canada

To Jill, nothing's quite as gratifying in the scrapbooking industry as being able to inspire others to create. That's why this stay-at-home mom and part-time University student always finds time for her hobby. Her passion started shortly after the birth of her son, Elijah, and has continued ever since.

maggie holmes
gilbert, arizona

Everything has a right place, according to organization-enthusiast, Maggie Holmes. In addition to scrapbooking, reading, interior decorating, exercising and being with family, she has recently found time to turn her passion for photography into a business. Despite her many projects, people tell her she's always smiling and happy. We believe it.

nia reddy
brooklyn, new york

Nia is a hunter and gatherer, browsing New York City for unique finds, great restaurants and whimsical letterpress cards. After six years of scrapbooking, she shows no signs of slowing down. In fact, Nia has been published in several national magazines and was the 2004 Hall of Fame winner. Currently, Nia resides in Brooklyn with her son Aiden and is looking to expand her family with the addition of a Boston Terrier.

christy tomlinson
shelley, idaho

Photographer, decorator, scrapbooker and mother. Christy manages to do it all and do it well. When she's not wrangling her six children, she can be found enjoying a novel or going to a late-night movie with her husband—in pajamas, naturally. Her motto, 'do what matters most', ensures she makes time to just sit back and laugh.

CONTRIBUTING ARTISTS

wendy bretz
ripley, new york

sherelle christensen
shelley, idaho

sharon eckles
salt lake city, utah

meghan olesen
phoenix, arizona

suzonne stirling
new orleans, louisiana

joey whittaker
salt lake city, utah

If fun is involved, count Joey in. This wife, mother and teacher is driven by everything delightful and laughs a lot. Whether she's playing the violin, disappearing into her music collection, or enjoying her dream home, Joey is loving life. Her interest in scrapbooking is derived from her need to create something worthwhile—and she did just that, becoming the latest MM Idol winner this past year. Congratulations!

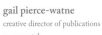

gail pierce-watne
creative director of publications
murray, utah

Some lives are just too big to be effectively capsulated in a measly paragraph. That's especially true of Gail. She runs big, with 18 marathons under her belt. She studies big, with a hard-earned Masters degree. And she scrapbooks big, creating projects that leave a lasting impression. In summary, landing Gail for our publications CD is kind of a big deal, no matter how short this paragraph may be.

BE inspired™